Wakefield Press

Being a Creature

Helen Parsons was born in Adelaide and has lived lived there all her life, apart from time spent studying in Italy and working in London.

Her poems have been published in Australian and international journals, and her collection *The Feeling of Bigness: Encountering Georgia O'Keeffe* was published in 2020 by Wakefield Press.

Being a Creature

THE CHRIST IN THE WILDERNESS PAINTINGS OF STANLEY SPENCER

HELEN PARSONS

Wakefield Press

Wakefield Press
16 Rose Street
Mile End
South Australia 5031

www.wakefieldpress.com.au

First published 2026

Designed and typeset by Michael Deves
Design development, artwork and cover design by Catherine Buddle
Printed by Finsbury Green, Adelaide SA

ISBN 978 1 92338 823 9

A catalogue record for this book is available from the National Library of Australia

Wakefield Press thanks Coriole Vineyards for their continued support

For my father

John Parsons

1924–2021

... when we love a work of art, there is always a form of recognition that occurs ... it answers something within us that we understand is true. The truth may be only a feeling, only a humming resonance we cannot put into words, or it may become a vast discursive statement, but it must be there for the enchantment to happen—that excursion into you that is also I.

Siri Hustvedt

Contents

Preface

I first saw Stanley Spencer's *Christ in the Wilderness* paintings more than forty years ago. I came upon them by chance as I wandered through the Art Gallery of Western Australia during a visit to Perth.

I was attracted by their warm glistening life, and struck by the sense of some mysterious and eccentric conviction underlying them. This Christ was not a refined transcendent figure but a heavy man, very much incarnate, and in close contact with the earth, its soil and stones, its plants and creatures.

I have seen the paintings again at intervals over the years, and have read much about Spencer's life and art. Through my daughter's friendship with Elspeth Pitt, now a senior curator at the National Gallery in Canberra, I learnt of the thesis she had written on these works during her student days.

Her study enabled me to see a much wider context for the paintings than just a particular time in Spencer's life. Elspeth argues that the paintings mark a transition in his spirituality, a move from a largely ritualistic sense of faith to a profoundly experiential one. I think she is right and that this is what gives the pictures their particular mystery and power.

Betty Churcher wrote that the purchase of these paintings by the Western Australian Gallery was a coup, and that we are very fortunate to have them here in Australia. I am grateful for the ways in which they have accompanied me in my life, ways which have found expression in these poems.

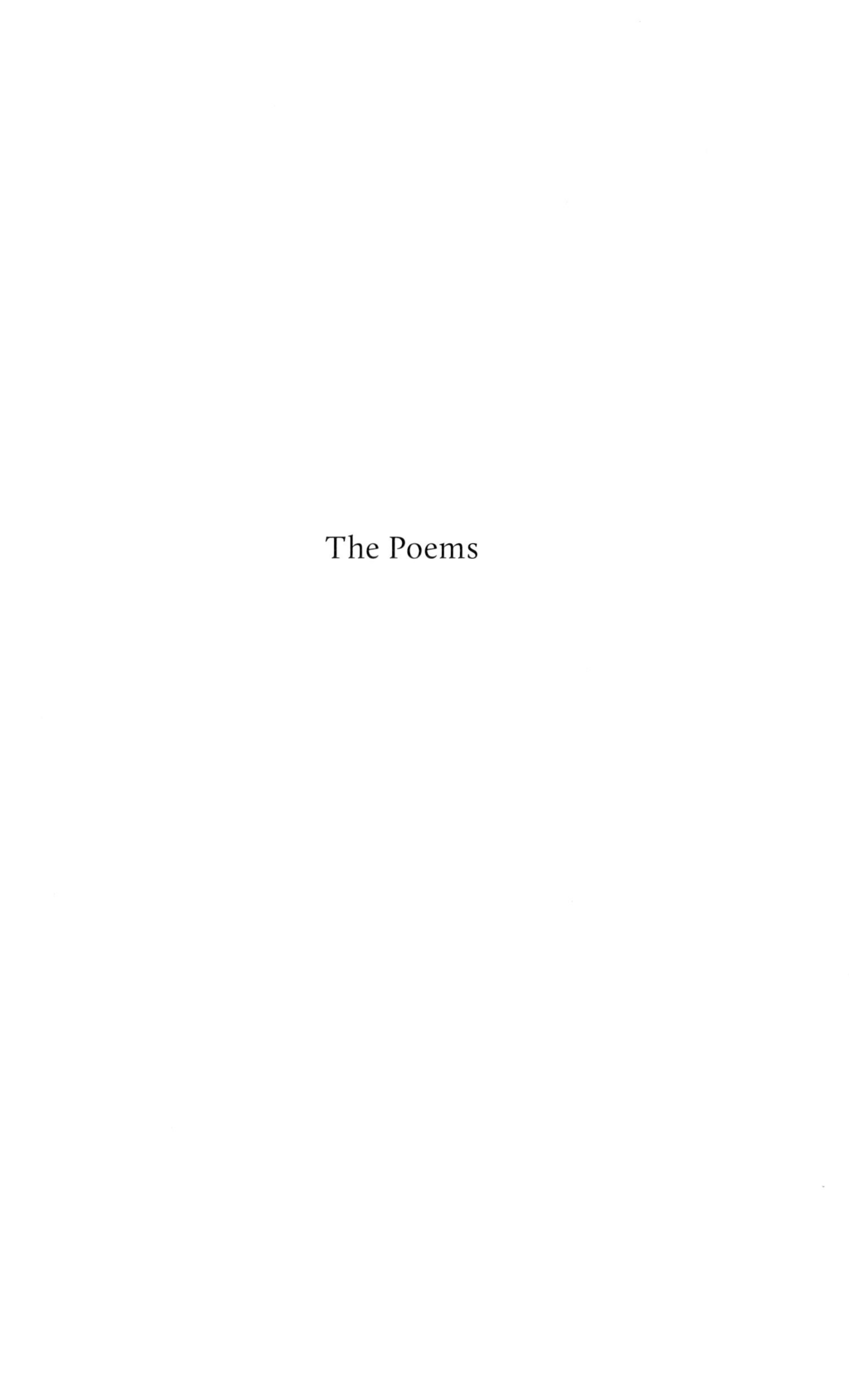

The Poems

Prologue

They come out of failure, these paintings,
which is why I love them ... Well,
one of the reasons. There are many.

Spencer's been foolish and he's been
betrayed. He's lost his family and his home,
is living in a kind of exile now.

Each day he sweeps his small bare room.
He needs the sustenance of ritual.
He needs the sustenance of art. He thinks

of Jesus in the wilderness, that chosen exile
of which we know so little. He invests it
with his feelings now and with his fund

of *memory-feelings*. The past resurfaces
and in his musings he returns to Macedonia,
those hills, that distant war, that early exile.

Meanwhile beyond his room a new war
looms and then begins. He's not the only one
who's made a mess of things.

Out in the London streets he sees
the Jewish refugees. In their dark eyes
lie depths of loss and lostness.

And so his Christ enters the wilderness.
He sits and kneels and lies upon the earth.
He grieves. He yearns. He ponders.

Stanley Spencer
Christ in the Wilderness: Driven by the spirit into the wilderness 1942
oil on canvas
56 x 56 cm
The State Art Collection, The Art Gallery of Western Australia
Purchased 1983

Driven

Stunted trees stand sparse on barren hills.
Christ steps across a ditch. He grasps a branch
to keep his balance, haul himself along.

I recognise the warrior pose I practise
in my yoga, in my life. It comforts me
to see his awkwardness, his firm resolve.

His gaze is forward but abstracted too,
drawn inward to the spirit driving him.
We don't go easily to the wilderness.

It is the alchemist's *nigredo* state,
a difficult disorienting passage.
It is necessity that drives us there.

As it had driven Spencer when he joined
the army all those years before, caught
in the current of the times, the grand romance.

Barracks was shock enough. Then came
the camps and trenches of a far-off land,
an alien terrain. But on the Salonika front

a line of hills reminded him of home.
He was remembering those hills,
he said, as he was painting this.

Perplexity is the path we travel on.
This sentence in the book I'm reading leaps
from the page at me. So calm about our lostness.

There he goes. Living his life. I'm sitting
on the porch beside my old vague father.
One of the local down-and-outs walks by,

a homeless man, enveloped in a mess
of layered garments, dirty big dark coat
and face-concealing hood. *There he goes*

my father says. *My friend. Living his life.*
He lifts a hand. It is as if one veteran
salutes another, and I'm wrenched back then

from seeing him as a victim, a lost soul.
He lives his life, and though the land he's in
strikes me with fear, seems comfortless,

he's right there in it, planting one bare foot
before the other, seizing a branch, a twig,
to help himself along. Living his life.

Am I talking of the street man or
my muddled dad? Both of them. And me.
And Spencer. And his human Christ.

Stanley Spencer
Christ in the Wilderness: Rising from sleep in the morning 1940
oil on canvas
56 x 56 cm
The State Art Collection, The Art Gallery of Western Australia
Purchased 1983

Rising

The grass emerges from amorphous dark,
each blade streaked with light. Christ rises too.
He's kneeling in a pit of corrugated clay.

His arms reach up, his robe spreads out around him,
sculpted like the chalk-white hills of Giotto.
It almost seems his body could be lifted

up from the earth, by faith, as Francis was
in the frescoes of the master Spencer loved.
But Stanley's Christ is earthbound. He has woken

in a crater like a soldier at the front,
and from this place he greets the dawning day,
the mutilated land, the healing grass.

There's something here about not being closed,
not staying curled and stuck and self-protective.
Something about the light, how we might meet it,

open to a sense of something bigger
and know that we are part of it. A faith.
The kind of faith I work towards each morning

with rituals of coffee, music, yoga.
The gas flares bright beneath the tarnished pot.
I listen for the bubbling to announce

day's bracing fresh infusion. Bach cantatas
give their infusion too of energy and grace.
I lift my arms and stretch, salute the sun.

But sometimes faith comes as a gift unbidden.
Perhaps you step out in the flush of dawn,
your mind abstracted, like a sailor sleeping

while his boat is entering new waters.
The sheets that you'd hung out the day before
are crisp and dry, chalk-white and deeply shadowed.

You reach up to unclip the wooden pegs.
You see the streaks of crimson in the east
and the vast curve of sky lit from below.

Like Stanley's Christ you pause
in wonderment. And then you take
into your arms the ordinary cloth,

carry the fullness back into the house,
as the sun rises and the light grows plain,
and the sky settles to its normal height.

Stanley Spencer
Christ in the Wilderness: The foxes have holes 1939
oil on canvas
56 x 56 cm
The State Art Collection, The Art Gallery of Western Australia
Purchased 1983

Foxes

A fox lifts up his tawny face towards the light.
Another slips into the darkness of his den.
Christ leans his back against the earthen bank

that houses them. Behind him ghost-pale roots
clutch barren ground. He is stretched out
around the foxes and their holes,

awkwardly settled, sombrely at peace.
He could be sitting with the paradox
of being at home in homelessness.

As Spencer sits with it inside his room,
and as he must have lived with it among
the trenches and the foxholes of the Front.

My father moves, is moved, into a Home
an institution for the aged. We crowd
his room with his old furniture, his pictures.

It's like the Tardis, says my brother when he enters.
But this Time Lord is lost, his memory fails.
Even the things of home cannot sustain him,

as neurones flicker and die out.
His window looks out on a big old gum,
all mass and up-reach and deep-rootedness.

My father always loved big trees.
When I resolved to have the lemon-scented
gum in my back yard cut down,

he cried instinctively that it would be
a crime. But I did cut it down although
it grieved me. Now he grieves me.

I wish that there could be a warm furred presence,
a dog to ground and reassure him
as these calm foxes reassure Christ,

and somehow comfort Spencer as he paints them,
soften the edges of his loneliness,
settle him and bring him down to earth.

Stanley Spencer
Christ in the Wilderness: He departed into a mountain to pray 1939
oil on canvas
56 x 56 cm
The State Art Collection, The Art Gallery of Western Australia
Purchased 1983

Prayer

I sit here at my desk. I'm stuck and helpless
with this poem. Unlike Spencer with these paintings.
He would sketch the outlines swiftly

and then fill them in with colour,
moving methodically across the canvas
like Giotto working on a chapel wall.

His Jesus kneels before a block of stone.
He puts his hands together like a child
and gazes upward, childlike, questioning.

I wonder whether Spencer looked like this
in this beleaguered period of his life.
It's how I often see my father look,

as he waits in his armchair in the Home,
his memory shot and no release in sight.
And my embattled youngest sister too,

when she's been bruised again
in her Asperger journey through the world.
It's how I sometimes feel. Defeated, lost,

longing to have some guidance, finding then
that most of all I need a place where I
can be with all of this and be received.

Is this what Christ is learning? Spencer too?
Can this be praying, the staying with confusion,
the bringing of it to a bigger space?

And then what happens?
When I got up just now and left my desk
and went down to the kitchen to make coffee,

the sketchy frog upon the painted plate
had come alive, and in the faded
and familiar postcard on the wall

the angel, phosphorescent, hurtled down
towards the dreaming emperor.
Such life. And so abundantly.

Stanley Spencer
Christ in the Wilderness: The scorpion 1939
oil on canvas
56 x 56 cm
The State Art Collection, The Art Gallery of Western Australia
Purchased 1983

Scorpion

Sometimes we have to repent. Sometimes
we have to walk a hundred miles
on our knees through the desert.

Sometimes we have to sit with it,
the damage that we do. Christ sits,
barefoot and heavy on the stony earth,

and in the grainy purgatorial light
he looks down at the scorpion poised upon
his unprotected palm. His face is shadowed.

He's seeing what it is to be a creature,
armoured and vulnerable, intricate,
instinctive. This is incarnation.

When I am sick with shame, when I've
misjudged, misunderstood, caused pain,
this painting comforts me. I want to flee

from this hard place, but Spencer stays,
and his Christ stays. I settle down with them,
share pain, find tenderness, go on.

Stanley Spencer
Christ in the Wilderness: Consider the lilies 1939
oil on canvas
56 x 56 cm
The State Art Collection, The Art Gallery of Western Australia
Purchased 1983

Lilies

He's on the ground, heavy on hands and knees,
massive, bulkier than the hills behind him.
He's marvelling at the lilies of the field.

He doesn't care how foolish he might look,
as Spencer never cared how he appeared
out in the world. He was unworldly, focused

on an inner realm: his store of memories,
and his Bible touchstones, all those tales
that had soaked into him in childhood.

Story meets with memory in him now:
his infant daughter crawling on the grass,
stopping to gaze upon a patch of flowers.

And so he paints his Christ down on the earth,
transfixed before some common village blooms.
Transparent, radiant and unimpeded,

that, says the teacher, is experience
if we accept un-knowing, leave
our managed lives, step out into the wild.

And so I take my coffee to the yard,
sit myself low upon the low stone wall,
stifle the impulses to smooth rough straw,

to snip a withered orange marigold.
And slowly mind goes quiet, gives up
its litany of tasks and shortfalls,

until there's just the stalks of marjoram
bearing their furred and fragrant leaves,
and the flax lily with its dark green blades

emerging braided from the earth.
A yellow shred of bamboo leaf drifts down
to float upon the coffee's dark brown pool.

A spider, smaller than a needle's eye,
circumnavigates a sun-warmed pot.

Stanley Spencer
Christ in the Wilderness: The eagles 1943
oil on canvas
56 x 56 cm
The State Art Collection, The Art Gallery of Western Australia
Purchased 1983

Eagles

Here Christ confronts the world as abattoir.
He's right down on the stony barren ground
where eagles tear the flesh from a dead deer.

So this is how it is. He looks away.
I cannot read his wide Byzantine eye.
I wonder how he comes to terms with this.

Spencer was down there too. He'd been
betrayed, and he had torn his family apart.
Deer and eagle, he was both of these.

There's something here of Christ Pantocrator
whose stern deep gaze from high mosaic domes
says life has laws that are inexorable.

Hard laws. And yet the deer's dead flesh
will feed the earth and fuel the eagles' flight.
And when the eagles lift into the sky

the sight will lift the heart, the hiding heart,
the heart that meets despair and guilt and hope,
the heart that stretches to contain them all.

Stanley Spencer
Christ in the Wilderness: The hen 1954
oil on canvas
57.2 x 58.1 cm
The State Art Collection, The Art Gallery of Western Australia
Purchased 1983

Hen

He shall neither slumber nor sleep,
declares the psalm of God's
protectiveness of us, a faith encoded

into the icon of *The Unsleeping Eye.*
A version of this icon hangs inside
a church in Macedonia, by the western door

for, as the psalm goes on to say, *The Lord*
shall keep thy going in and coming out.
Did Spencer come and go and see this image?

His Christ is lying in the same curved posture.
He supports his heavy head in the same way
and watches. Does not slumber. Does not sleep.

But some time he will have to sleep, of course.
His eyes look weary now, one's almost closed.
His big recumbent body makes a levee

and the hen is there inside, her warm
brown feathers offering to her chicks
a dusty safety. Haven within a haven.

But hurricanes sweep in and levees crumble.
There's no safety in the end. We know this.
Not for ourselves and not for those we love.

Our father's moving ineluctably
into the clouded realms. He knows
he's going there. He visited his sister

through her last lost years. He's always been
the one who visited, the one who cared.
As a boy he'd sit beside his mother

and read to her as she lay on the couch,
the rheumatoid arthritis tightening its grip
and taking her at last when he was twelve.

I look at Spencer's Christ. A weariness
is etched into the straight line of his mouth.
Here in the wilderness he's up against

our human limits, learning like us to feel
and not to be undone by feeling. To do
what can be done. To be a presence.

Stanley Spencer
Christ in the Wilderness: The foxes have holes c1938–c1939
pencil on paper
26.4 x 26.3 cm
The State Art Collection, The Art Gallery of Western Australia
Purchased 1983

Epilogue

Spencer dreamed of painting forty pictures,
one for each day in the wilderness.
He sketched them all. He finished only eight.

His path led him away from his first vision,
then drew him back, and drew him back again,
and finally away. When he began

he had imagined them fixed high
upon the ceiling of a village church,
so the parishioners could lift their eyes

and through the dimness see their Christ
deep in his earthly life. But here they are,
as far from Cookham as they could have gone,

and in a sunlit public gallery.
There I first saw them forty years ago.
They drew me to them, touched me,

stayed with me, held meanings that I needed.
In them puzzlement was a place to rest in,
grace could co-exist with awkwardness,

and the human being was part of nature,
not separate from the fox, the scorpion,
the rising sun, the lilies of the field.

What is art for? A broken cup, said Frost,
the plaything of a child, but you can fill it
with water from the spring, drink, and be whole.

Spencer filled a cup to meet his thirst.
In the browns and greens of earth and grass,
in Christ's voluminous chalk-coloured robes,

his heavy body, naked feet, dark gaze,
and in the barren contours of the hills,
he found a way to pray, to be consoled.

The work's unfinished, but this cup is here,
connecting us to him and to the springs.
I drink. I fill my broken cup. I thank him.

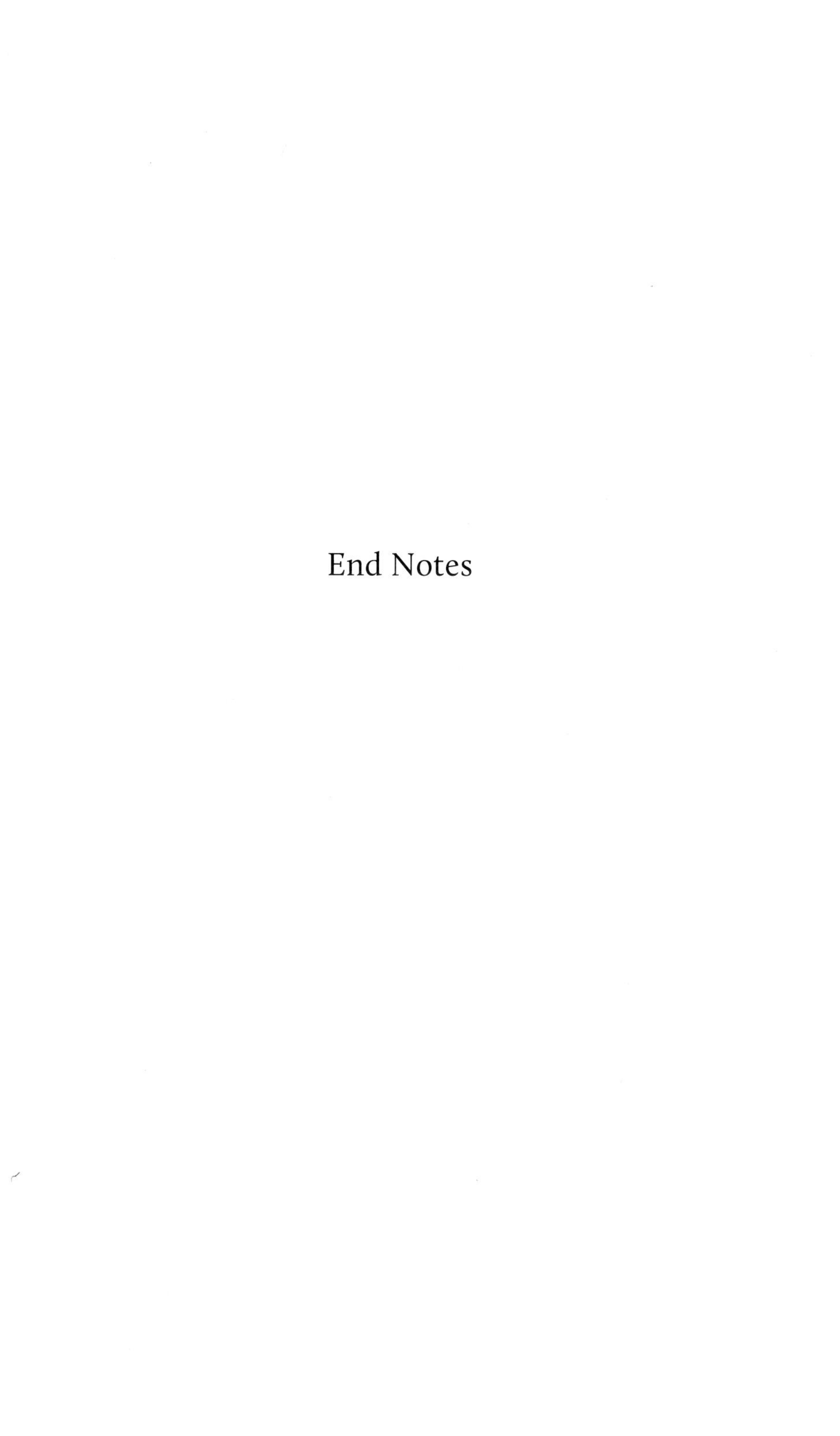

End Notes

Notes on the Paintings

These verses from the King James Bible accompanied the reproductions of Stanley Spencer's *Christ in the Wilderness* series of paintings in the catalogue from the London Royal Academy of Art 1980 exhibition:

Page 7
Driven by the spirit into the wilderness 1942
'And immediately the Spirit driveth him into the wilderness.' Mark 1:12

Page 11
Rising from sleep in the morning 1940
'I will arise and go to my Father.' Luke 15:18

Page 15
The foxes have holes 1939
'... the foxes have holes and the birds of the air have nests; but the Son of man hath not where to lay his head.' Matthew 8:20

Page 19
He departed into a mountain to pray 1939
'And when he had sent them away he departed into a mountain to pray.' Mark 6:46

Page 23

The scorpion 1939

'Behold, I give unto you the power to tread on serpents and scorpions, and over all the power of the enemy: and nothing shall by any means hurt you.' Luke 10:19

Page 27

Consider the lilies 1939

'Consider the lilies of the field, how they grow; they toil not, neither do they spin; And yet I say unto you, that even Solomon in all his glory was not arrayed like one of these.' Matthew 6: 28–29

Page 31

The eagles 1943

'For wheresoever the carcase is, there will the eagles be gathered together.' Matthew 24:28

Page 35

The hen 1954

'... how often would I have gathered my children together, even as a hen gathereth her chickens under her wings ...' Matthew 23:37

Piero della Francesca
The Legend of the True Cross: The Dream of Constantine c1466
fresco,329 x 190 cm
Basilica di San Francesco, Arezzo

Notes on the Poems

Prologue

They come out of failure

By the end of 1938 Spencer had lost his family and his home and was in desperate financial circumstances. This had come about through his obsession, since 1931, with the artist Patricia Preece. Spencer had pursued Patricia intensely, and wanted his wife Hilda to include her in their marriage. Hilda eventually, with their two daughters, left him, and they were divorced in 1937. Immediately after the divorce Stanley married Patricia. However the marriage was not consummated and Stanley was forced to leave his house, which Patricia had earlier persuaded him to sign over to her.

memory-feelings

Spencer often spoke of his 'memory-feelings', by which he meant the assemblages of memories and emotions that formed the basis of his paintings.

Macedonia

Spencer joined the army in July 1915. After serving for thirteen months as a hospital orderly in Beaufort War Hospital, Bristol, he was transferred abroad and spent the next two and a half years in Macedonia.

Giotto di Bondone
The Legend of St Francis: The Ecstasy of St Francis 1297–1300
fresco
270 x 230 cm
Upper Church, San Francesco, Assisi

Driven

Perplexity is the path we travel on
'This perplexed questioning is the central path itself.'
Stephen Batchelor *Buddhism Without Beliefs* page 98

Rising

as Francis was
The ecstasy of St Francis in *The Legend of St Francis*, Giotto, fresco 1297–1300 Upper Church, San Francesco, Assisi.

Foxes

the Front
In Macedonia Spencer served initially in the Field Ambulance divisions, but in August 1917 he volunteered for the infantry, and spent several months in the front line as Private Spencer.

somehow comfort Spencer
Talking about this painting Spencer said later: 'It is a sort of "placeless" place. You are in a sort of nowhere and nowhere is not home, and this making a double home—one for the foxes and one for Christ—brings about a homely feeling that I want without altering anything else in Nature.'
Stephen Cottrell *Christ in the Wilderness: Reflecting on the paintings by Stanley Spencer* page 69, quoting from Spencer's reflections in 1950, held in the archives of the Stanley Spencer Gallery in Cookham

Christ Pantocrator
dome mosaic c1080–1100
Church of the Formation
Monastery of Daphni, Greece

Prayer

the angel ... the dreaming emperor
The work referred to is Piero della Francesca's *The Dream of Constantine.* Constantine is asleep and about to be visited by an angel who appears in the top left corner in a dramatic effect of backlighting.

Such life. And so abundantly
'I am come that they might have life, and that they might have it more abundantly.' John 10:10 King James Bible

Scorpion

Sometimes we have to repent
This references the opening lines of Mary Oliver's poem *Wild Geese.*

Lilies

Transparent, radiant and unimpeded
Stephen Batchelor *Buddhism Without Beliefs* page 98

Eagles

Christ Pantocrator
In Christian iconography, Christ Pantocrator is a depiction of Christ as all-powerful, literally the ruler of all. It is one of the most common images of Eastern Orthodox Christianity.

the hiding heart
This phrase echoes Gerard Manley Hopkins in his sonnet *The Windhover*: My heart in hiding/ Stirred for a bird, the achieve of; the mastery of the thing!

mid-14th century icon
Monastery of John the Forerunner
Serres, Greece

Hen

a church in Macedonia
The facing page shows the mid-14th century icon held in the Monastery of John the Forerunner, a few miles from Serres in northern Greece.

Epilogue

Spencer dreamed of painting forty pictures
In his initial planning for the series, Spencer drew up a grid, based on the ceiling of the chancel of the Holy Trinity Church, Cookham, and made a thumbnail sketch of each of the panels in position.

a sunlit public gallery
The paintings and sketches were purchased by the Art Gallery of Western Australia in 1983.

A broken cup
The lines cited are from Robert Frost's poem 'Directive'.

Bibliography

Batchelor, Stephen *Buddhism Without Beliefs: A contemporary guide to awakening.* London, Bloomsbury, 1997

Churcher, Betty *Australian Notebooks.* Melbourne, The Miegunyah Press, 2014

Cottrell, Stephen *Christ in the Wilderness: Reflecting on the paintings by Stanley Spencer.* London, Society for Promoting Christian Knowledge, 2012

Harpley, Melissa in Ted Gott et al., *Modern Britain 1900-1960: Masterworks from Australian and New Zealand Collections.* Melbourne, National Gallery of Victoria, 2007

MacCarthy, Fiona *Stanley Spencer An English Vision.* New Haven, Yale University Press, 1997

Pitt, Elspeth 'From the Ritualistic to the Experiential: The evolution of an artist's spirituality as portrayed in Stanley Spencer's Christ in the Wilderness paintings.' Dissertation submitted in partial fulfilment of the degree of Master of Arts (Studies in Art History,) History Department, University of Adelaide, December 2008

Pople, Kenneth *Stanley Spencer: A Biography.* London, Collins, 1991

The epigraph is from Siri Hustvedt's essay 'Embodied Visions' in *Living, Thinking, Looking.* New York, Picador, 2012, page 53

Acknowledgements

I am grateful to Elspeth Pitt, currently Senior Curator of Australian Art at the Australian National Gallery, for giving me access to her illuminating thesis on the *Christ in the Wilderness* paintings.

Thank you to Diane Fahey and to Jan Owen, mentors over many years, for their helpful feedback and their encouragement.

And to other poet friends for their support, especially Jan Andrews, Maggie Slattery, Louise Nicholas, Heather Nimmo, and Helen Lindstrom.

To my sister Hilary and my daughter Annie and my dear friend Sue for their abiding faith.

To Narelle McKenzie, Bob Gibson and Pam Evers for their various gifts.

To Michael Deves for his invaluable help in the publication process.

And to Catherine Buddle for applying her formidable artistry to the design of this small book.

Wakefield Press is an independent publishing and
distribution company based in Adelaide, South Australia.
We love good stories and publish beautiful books.
To see our full range of books, please visit our website at
www.wakefieldpress.com.au
where all titles are available for purchase.
To keep up with our latest releases and news,
subscribe to the *Wakefield Weekly* at
https://mailchi.mp/wakefieldpress/subscribe

Find us!

Facebook: www.facebook.com/wakefield.press
Instagram: www.instagram.com/wakefieldpress